D0549018

# Allergies

ANN O. SQUIRE

**Children's Press®**
An Imprint of Scholastic Inc.

**Content Consultant**

Karen E. Peters, DrPH
Clinical Assistant Professor
Division of Community Health Sciences
School of Public Health
University of Illinois—Chicago
Chicago, Illinois

Library of Congress Cataloging-in-Publication Data
Squire, Ann O.
  Allergies / by Ann O. Squire.
    pages cm. — (A true book)
  Includes bibliographical references and index.
  ISBN 978-0-531-21470-1 (library binding : alk. paper) — ISBN 978-0-531-21520-3 (pbk. : alk.
paper)
1. Allergy—Juvenile literature. 2. Allergy in children—Juvenile literature. I. Title.
  RC585.S65 2016
  618.92'97—dc23                                      2014046959

**Front cover: A girl blowing her
nose in a field of wildflowers**

**Back cover: EpiPens**

# Find the Truth!

**Everything** you are about to read is true *except* for one of the sentences on this page.

Which one is **TRUE**?

**T or F** Once someone has an allergy, he or she has it for life. It will never go away.

**T or F** If a child's parents have allergies, that child is more likely to have allergies as well.

Find the answers in this book.

3

# Contents

**EpiPen**

## THE BIG TRUTH!

## Anaphylaxis

What happens when a person
experiences anaphylaxis? ................. 18

Plant pollen is a common allergy trigger in the springtime.

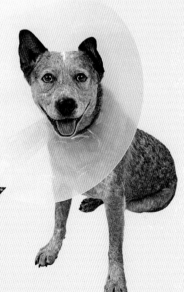

Both people and pets can suffer from allergies.

5

# CHAPTER 1

# What Can It Be?

It was lunchtime in Mrs. Johnson's kindergarten class. Natalie, one of the younger students, had taken a few bites of her sandwich and put it down. Mrs. Johnson noticed what looked like small bumps around the girl's mouth. Natalie was scratching her face, and she seemed to be having trouble breathing. Worried, Mrs. Johnson picked up the phone and called the school nurse.

 Food allergies are more common in children than in adults.

# Finding the Cause

When Natalie reached the nurse's office, her throat was feeling tight. It was difficult to breathe. Her face felt itchy, and her stomach hurt. The nurse gave her some water. After drinking it, Natalie felt a little better. The nurse called Natalie's mom, who arrived right away. The nurse had questions for her. Had Natalie felt well that morning? Had she recently been sick? Did she have any health problems or allergies?

**School nurses take care of students if they become sick at school.**

8

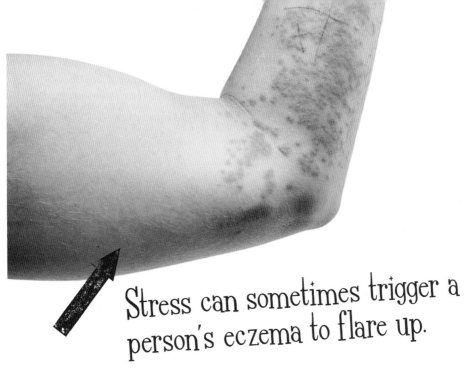

Stress can sometimes trigger a person's eczema to flare up.

Natalie had been feeling fine. She had never been allergic to anything. However, she did have **eczema** (EK-suh-muh). This condition often made Natalie's skin dry, flaky, and irritated. The doctor had given her a prescription, or written order, for a cream to help. He also told her to avoid substances that might irritate her skin. These included harsh soaps, fabric softeners, and perfumes. Natalie's dad had allergies to some of those things. So her mom was used to keeping them out of the house.

**Many people around the world suffer from severe peanut allergies.**

# Food Allergies

The nurse wondered if something in Natalie's lunch had caused her symptoms. Natalie had brought a peanut butter sandwich for lunch. It was after she started eating it that she had begun feeling bad. Peanuts are a common allergen, or substance that causes an allergic reaction. Peanut allergies can cause very serious, sometimes life-threatening, reactions. Knowing this, the nurse urged Natalie's mom to take her daughter to the doctor.

# Lifesaving Dogs

For people with food allergies, every meal is a possible danger. Accidentally eating food containing an allergen can cause a life-threatening reaction. Some people react just by inhaling (breathing in) an allergen. Fortunately, some people can depend on an allergy-alert dog to help keep them safe. A dog's sense of smell is much better than a human's. A dog can be trained to sniff out a specific food allergen, whether the food is cooked, raw, or mixed with other foods.

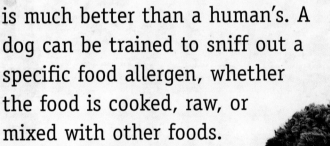

Doctors ask their
patients questions
to better understand
what might be wrong.

# CHAPTER 2

# Making a Diagnosis

After talking to the family doctor, Natalie's mom made an appointment with an **allergist**. The allergist started by asking if Natalie had been sick recently, if she had any health conditions, and if she had ever had an allergic reaction to any type of food. He was interested to learn about Natalie's eczema. He explained that many children with eczema develop food allergies. Sensitivities to peanuts, milk, wheat, soy, and eggs are among the most common.

Roughly one in five Americans have allergy symptoms.

# Testing for Allergies

The doctor considered doing an allergy scratch test. In this test, a number of light scratches are made on a patient's skin. Then, drops of liquid containing different allergens are placed on the scratches. After a short time, the doctor checks the skin for swelling and redness. This would indicate an allergy. But Natalie had sensitive skin and eczema. The doctor worried that this test might irritate her skin further, so he decided against it.

**When doing a scratch test, doctors label the location of each allergen on a patient's body.**

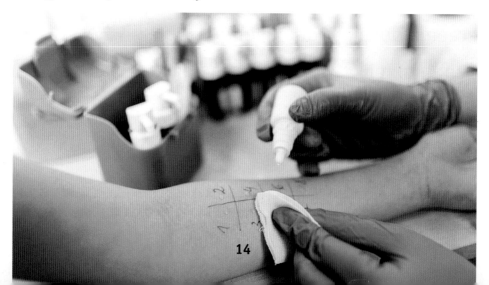

14

**A close look at a patient's blood can reveal a lot of information about his or her health.**

## Blood Test

There are other ways to test for an allergy. Natalie's doctor decided to do a blood test. After drawing a blood sample, he sent it to a lab to test for **antibodies** to peanuts and other foods. A person's body produces antibodies in response to threats such as bacteria, viruses, and allergens. It usually takes a few days to get the results. The doctor said to be sure Natalie avoided peanuts until they had the answer.

Someone with a nut allergy avoids nuts in any form, even if they are baked into food.

The following week, the doctor called with the results. Natalie's blood had antibodies to peanuts and several other nuts. The antibodies strongly indicated that she had allergies to these substances. The doctor said that Natalie shouldn't eat any foods containing the suspected allergens. He asked her mom to call the office in a few weeks to check in. If Natalie avoided nuts and had no symptoms, it would be another clue that she was allergic to them.

# Food Challenge Test

In a food challenge test, the person eats a very small amount of the suspected food. A doctor watches for an allergic reaction. If there is no reaction, a larger amount is given. If the person shows any sign of a reaction, the test is stopped. The doctor gives medications to stop the symptoms. Food challenge tests are very accurate. However, they must be performed in a medical setting in case of a serious reaction.

**Doctors can use a food challenge test with a patient of any age.**

# Anaphylaxis

Many allergies cause sneezing, a runny nose, and watery eyes. These symptoms can be annoying. But some allergies can be downright dangerous. These include allergies to foods, insect stings and bites, certain medicines, and latex, a material used in rubber gloves. Such allergens can cause a severe reaction called anaphylaxis (an-uh-fih-LAK-sis).

In anaphylaxis, the body releases many chemicals very quickly. The chemicals cause a person's heart to slow

18

down and the pulse and body to become weak. The person may also become dizzy, and breathing becomes difficult. If it is not treated immediately, anaphylaxis can be fatal.

For people at risk of anaphylaxis, a doctor prescribes an epinephrine (eh-puh-NEF-rin) injector. This is usually called an EpiPen. It is used when a person begins to have anaphylactic symptoms. It provides medicine to help relieve the symptoms.

After using an EpiPen, a person should always visit an emergency room. This allows doctors and nurses to make sure the symptoms don't return. Patients who have an EpiPen always carry it with them and know how to use it. It could save their life!

# CHAPTER 3

# Why Is a Person Allergic?

Natalie's mom felt terrible. She wondered why her daughter had become allergic. Was there anything she could have done to prevent it? The doctor explained that allergies are very common. In fact, up to 60 million people in the United States are allergic to something. Allergies can develop at any age, even before birth! Some allergies last a lifetime, while others may go away as the person grows up.

 Allergies to grass and other plants are generally not severe enough to cause anaphylaxis.

# An Allergic Family

The tendency to have allergies seems to run in families. If neither of your parents has an allergy, you have only a 15 percent chance of developing one. If one parent is allergic, your chances are about 30 percent. If both parents are, your chances rise to 60 percent. People don't inherit any particular allergy, just the tendency to become allergic. Relatives will not necessarily all have the same allergies.

**One member of a family may be allergic to milk and need to avoid it, while other members can drink milk but must avoid other substances.**

22

**People with pets sometimes develop allergies to the animals.**

# Allergens in the Environment

An inherited tendency to have allergies is just
half of the story. To become allergic, you have
to be exposed to allergens and irritants in the
environment. If you are not exposed to something,
you will not become allergic to it. For example, if you
never eat peanuts, you will never show symptoms of
a peanut allergy. A person needs to have repeated
contact with something to become allergic to it.

Allergic reactions to dust or pollen are sometimes called hay fever.

## What Exactly Is an Allergy?

To understand allergies, we need to understand the **immune system**. This is a network of cells, organs, and tissues in the body. It keeps a person healthy by attacking "invaders" such as germs and viruses. When the immune system detects a substance that should not be present, it produces antibodies to attack the invader. The sneezing, coughing, and runny nose of a cold are all signs that the immune system is fighting a cold virus.

For many people, the immune system works just fine. But in people with allergies, the immune system becomes confused. It mistakes harmless substances such as pollen or pet **dander** for alien invaders. In response, the immune system produces a type of antibody called immunoglobulin E (IgE). The IgE antibodies attach to cells in the body. When an allergen is present, the antibodies tell the cells to release a substance called histamine. Histamine is what causes allergy symptoms.

**IgE antibodies attach to mast cells like this one, telling it to release histamines whenever a certain allergen is present.**

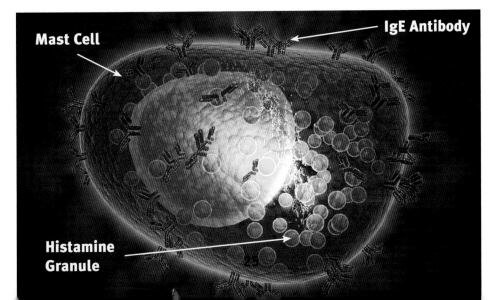

Mast Cell

IgE Antibody

Histamine Granule

# Repeated Exposure

When you first come into contact with an allergen, you will probably not react. That is because the immune system has not yet produced antibodies against it. Once antibodies have been produced, they stay in the body, ready to spring into action. Each time you are exposed to a particular allergen, more antibodies are manufactured. Before long, you have a full-blown allergy. It will take very little to trigger an allergic response.

**Allergies develop and worsen over time. Each time a person allergic to peanuts comes into contact with a peanut, the reaction is more severe.**

**Ragweed pollen is a common allergen in the fall, when the plant blooms.**

# Specific Antibodies

Why are some people allergic to pets and others to pollen? Why aren't people with allergies sensitive to everything? The answer lies in the IgE antibodies produced by the immune system. Just like a key that opens a specific lock, each antibody is designed to work on only one specific allergen. So even if a person is allergic to ragweed pollen, there's a good chance that pets or dust won't affect that person at all.

STEAMED LEMON POT

# GLUTEN
# AND BROWNIE LEMON
# DAIRY DRIZZLE ALMOND
# FREE TART CARROT
# CAKES CAKE OR
# MUFFINS
## IT'S GOOD.

# Treating Allergies

Let's say you have just been **diagnosed** with an allergy. What can you do to avoid suffering allergy symptoms? The most effective treatment is to stay away from the substance that triggers the allergy. In the case of a food allergy like Natalie's, this seems pretty simple: don't eat peanuts or other nuts that provoke a reaction. Sometimes, however, nuts and other food allergens pop up where people least expect them.

Many restaurants offer special menu choices for patrons with food allergies.

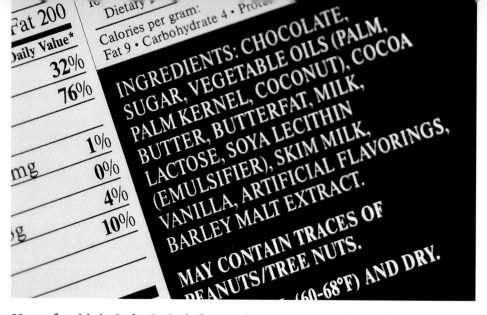

**Many food labels include information about possible allergens in the product.**

# "Hidden" Peanuts

Peanuts and other nuts can show up in baked goods, packaged breads, ice cream, granola bars, candy, and more. Even salad dressings and pet foods can contain traces of nuts. If you have an allergy to nuts or some other type of food, it is very important to read food labels. Food manufacturers are required to list every ingredient that goes into a product, no matter how small the amount.

# Cross-Contamination

Even if a product does not contain an allergen, it may have picked up traces if it was prepared or manufactured in a place where that allergen was present. Again, it's important to read the label. Look for statements such as "produced on equipment shared with nuts or peanuts." For people with severe food allergies, it takes only a tiny amount to bring about a reaction.

**Multiple foods might be produced in the same factory or on the same equipment.**

31

# Avoiding Cross-Contamination at Home

For people who have food allergies, the best plan is to keep the food out of the house altogether. But that's not always possible. The next best thing is to be extra careful in the kitchen. Family members should wash all utensils and their hands in hot, soapy water after preparing food. Even cutting boards, toasters, pots, and pans can carry small traces of allergenic foods. When visiting a restaurant, a person should let the servers know about a food allergy.

**Clean dishes can cut down on the possibility of spreading a food allergy.**

Millions of dust mites are living in your bed right now!

## Other Allergens

With allergens in the air, such as mold or dust mites, an extra-clean home can help. Dust mites are very small creatures that live in dust. One way to reduce them is to make the home free of "dust-catchers" such as rugs and curtains. The bedroom usually has the most dust mites. People can control them there by keeping the mattress and pillows in allergy-proof coverings. Washing the sheets regularly in hot water also helps.

# Pet and Seasonal Allergies

What if people are allergic to their cat or dog? Finding the pet a new home is the most effective solution. Other options include keeping the pet out of the bedroom to control allergens there. Bathing the pet, its toys, and its bedding regularly also helps. So does keeping the home clean and free of pet hair. Air filters and air cleaners help clear pet dander and hair from the air.

Millions of people have allergies that flare up in spring, when flowering trees and plants release their pollen. Many people find relief by taking antihistamines. These medicines work against the body's histamines. A doctor might also prescribe a nasal spray that reduces **inflammation**. Decongestants reduce the stuffiness in a person's nose. These medicines can help with dust and pet allergies, too.

# Common Seasonal Allergies

## Winter
Indoor allergies such as mold, pet dander, and dust cause the biggest problems. Pine trees during Christmastime can also trigger a reaction.

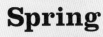

## Spring
Tree and grass pollen are at their highest.

## Fall
Ragweed is the most common fall allergy. Outdoor molds are also still present.

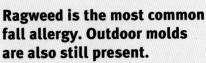

## Summer
Outdoor molds and spores fill the air.

Immunotherapy may help prevent certain new allergies from developing.

## Allergen Immunotherapy

Allergen immunotherapy is a fancy term for allergy shots. This is another way of treating allergies. An allergy shot contains a tiny amount of an allergen. There is enough of the allergen to trigger a person's immune system but not enough to cause a reaction. Over time, the amount of allergen in each shot is increased. Eventually, a person's immune system builds up a tolerance. This means it becomes used to the substance and reacts less strongly.

# Sticking With It

Allergy shots can be very effective, but the process is lengthy and you need to stick with it. The first phase is buildup. A patient receives shots once or twice a week, gradually increasing the amount of the allergen. This phase lasts for several months. The next phase is maintenance. A patient receives shots less often to maintain the body's tolerance to the allergen. Allergy shots work best for people sensitive to pollen, dust mites, and bee stings.

**It can take several months of immunotherapy for patients to notice a change in their allergies.**

It takes years of research and testing to develop a new medicine.

# CHAPTER 5

# New Advances in Allergy Treatment

Allergies have been around forever. But recent advances promise to make life easier for people with allergies. Scientists have developed pills that work the same way as allergy shots. Instead of making repeated trips to the allergist for shots, a patient simply takes a pill. So far, only pills that work against grass pollen are available, but more are in the works. To be effective, the medication must be started several months before the pollen season begins.

# Improving Immunotherapy

Until recently, immunotherapy has not been used for food allergies. Patients with severe food allergies often live in fear of accidentally eating a small amount of the food that causes the reaction. But scientists have been experimenting with oral immunotherapy on patients with peanut allergies. They start with tiny amounts of peanut and increase the amounts over time.

**Oral immunotherapy might someday help patients worry less about a food's ingredients.**

**Early in an immunotherapy program to overcome peanut allergies, a patient might eat just a single peanut a day.**

The researchers were excited with the results. People in the study became much less sensitive to peanuts. Because reactions to a peanut allergy can be life threatening, these findings are great news for people allergic to peanuts. However, this improvement in their allergy must be maintained. That means the patients will probably have to eat peanuts every day for the rest of their lives.

New, more effective allergy treatments might mean people no longer have to worry about plant pollen and other allergens.

## Keeping IgE Low

Scientists are also working on a new inhaled drug to block the production of the IgE antibody. In tests, allergic patients who took the drug had lower levels of IgE. What's more, these levels remained low for up to a month. Soon, it may be possible to manage allergies by inhaling the drug once every few months! With such medicines in development, allergy treatments will become easier and more effective.

# Can Cats and Dogs Have Allergies?

Pets are often sensitive to the same allergens that affect people. Pollen, mold, dust, smoke, and certain medicines are just a few examples. Pets may show similar symptoms, including sneezing, coughing, watery eyes, and itchy skin. If your pet has a food allergy, it may scratch at its face or have problems with vomiting and diarrhea. Pets can even be allergic to fleas. If you think your dog or cat has allergies, talk to a veterinarian.

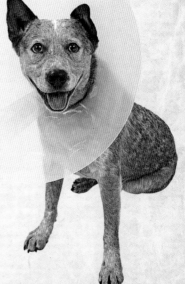

**Percent of children in the United States with food allergies:** 8

**Number of school-age children in the United States who have a peanut allergy:** 400,000

**Percent of children with food allergies who are sensitive to more than one food:** More than 30

**Percent of people in the United States who test positive for at least one allergy:** 55

**Percent of people in the United States with an allergy to latex:** Less than 1

**Percent of health care workers with an allergy to latex:** 8 to 17

**Number of dust mites living in the average bed:** Between 1 and 10 million

# Did you find the truth?

**(F)** Once someone has an allergy, he or she has it for life. It will never go away.

**(T)** If a child's parents have allergies, that child is more likely to have allergies as well.

# Resources

## Books

Hammond, Leslie, and Lynne Marie Rominger. *Allergy Proof Recipes for Kids: More Than 150 Recipes That Are All Wheat-Free, Gluten-Free, Nut-Free, Egg-Free, Dairy-Free, and Low in Sugar.* Beverly, MA: Fair Winds Press, 2010.

Simons, Rae. *What Causes Allergies?* Vestal, NY: Village Earth Press, 2012.

Taylor-Butler, Christine. *Food Allergies*. New York: Children's Press, 2008.

**Visit this Scholastic Web site for more information on allergies:**
★ www.factsfornow.scholastic.com
Enter the keyword **Allergies**

# Important Words

**allergist** (AL-ur-jist) — a doctor who specializes in diagnosing and treating allergies

**anaphylaxis** (an-uh-fih-LAK-sis) — a severe, potentially fatal bodily reaction to a substance a person is allergic to

**antibodies** (AN-ti-bah-deez) — substances produced by the body to fight off foreign invaders such as viruses, bacteria, or allergens

**dander** (DAN-dur) — tiny scales from hair, feathers, or skin that can cause allergies

**diagnosed** (dye-uhg-NOHSD) — determined what disease a person has or what the cause of a problem is

**eczema** (EG-zuh-muh) — a medical condition that makes the skin dry, rough, and itchy

**epinephrine** (eh-puh-NEF-rin) — a fast-acting medicine used in emergencies to treat serious allergic reactions

**immune system** (i-MYOON SIS-tuhm) — the system that protects the body against disease and infection

**inflammation** (in-fluh-MAY-shuhn) — redness, swelling, heat, and pain usually caused by an infection, injury, or allergic reaction

# Index

Page numbers in **bold** indicate illustrations.

# About the Author

Ann O. Squire is a psychologist and an animal behaviorist. Before becoming a writer, she studied the behavior of rats, tropical fish in the Caribbean, and electric fish from central Africa. Her favorite part of being a writer is the chance to learn as much as she can about all sorts of topics. In addition to *Allergies* and books on other health topics, Dr. Squire has written about many different animals, from lemmings to leopards and cicadas to cheetahs. She lives in Long Island City, New York.